Layers Unleashed

7 Layers of Unleashing The Inner You

MJ Roberson

MJ Roberson

Layers Unleashed

Copyright © 2018 by Monica Roberson.

All rights reserved.

No part of this book may be reproduced or transmitted in any form or by any means, electronic or mechanical, including photocopying, recording, or by any information storage and retrieval system, without permission in writing from the copyright author, except for the use of brief quotations in a book review.

ISBN: 978-1-970135-01-5 hardcover
       978-1-970135-02-2 paperback
       978-1-970135-03-9 eBook

Published in the United States by Pen2Pad Ink Publishing www.pen2padink.org.

Requests to publish work from this book or to contact the author should be sent to: layersunleashed4u@gmail.com

Monica Roberson retains the rights to all images.

MJ Roberson

Contents

LAYER 1
Unleashing The Layers of Trauma
Pg. 11

LAYER 2
Unleashing The Layers of Family
Pg. 25

LAYER 3
Unleashing The Layers of Marriage
Pg. 42

LAYER 4
Unleashing The Layers of Finances
Pg. 59

LAYER 5
Unleashing The Layers of Friendships
Pg. 74

LAYER 6
Unleashing The Layers of Children
Pg. 88

LAYER 7
Unleashing The Layers of the Tongue
Pg. 99

Message From the Author
Pg. 106

MJ Roberson

Acknowledgements

I would like to first thank God for being my number one confidant. He has instilled in me wisdom and the experience needed to endure any obstacle or trial that I've faced for the last 32 years.

To my parents, I can't thank you enough for giving birth to me. I've become a courageous young woman who may have bent, but never broke throughout this beautiful life. Many times, I've questioned why this life was chosen for me, but it has given me a greater meaning and destiny. The love I have for you is unconditional.

To my Husband, you were and are a breath of fresh air to my life even in our rough moments. As the famous Yolanda Adams said, "Nobody told me it would be easy," and we have experienced that phase. I've lived a life that you can only half understand. Each year however, you've been able to uncover an additional piece within me. The road will only get better. I love you to life!

To my one and only Prince Jamyreon. Though you may not understand why you are here on earth, I will always be here to remind you. In life you have to learn that as an adult, you have to make adult decisions. Sometimes making these decisions can be hard, but the best one I made was giving life to you. You have taught me how to be strong and to fight when the fight was almost gone. You showed me how to keep a job, how to be a mother, and love someone even when I had no clue how to love myself. Remember that no matter who may give up on you or leave your side, you will always have me!

To my one and only Princess Acelynn, mommy was so excited to find out that "It's a Girl." You have brought me joy and you are an image of me. You are strong and feisty, but we all know where you get that. It is a blessing and honor to call you my "mini me."

To my siblings Tedril & Deshone, I love you both more than you'll ever know and that's to life. Over the years, I know we haven't had the bond I imagined or dreamed of. However, no matter what, I am my sister's keeper. We are three bright, strong and courageous women who have all had to learn how to get what we needed. We did it the best way we knew how with the cards that were dealt to us! It may not have been the AKQ of spades, but it was a unique set of cards that helped us endure the struggle and journey of life. I'm thankful for you being in my life.

To my family and friends who have supported me through this journey of life and writing my very first book. Thank you for your continuous love, support and words of encouragement. Your efforts are never underappreciated. Remember you too, can live your dreams and bring your vision to life by drafting a plan and taking the steps to put them into action.

"If you lack in your process, it will hinder your progress"

- MJ Roberson

Introduction

There are many times when things go wrong in life. Know that these trials and tribulations come to build up your strength for the journey that awaits you. The burdens placed upon you are not there to kill you, but to help you develop the tenacity and enduring power to establish a life worth living. If everything was perfect, life would not have meaning. Most of us try to hide these mishaps in the back of our mind and never pick them back up, thinking we can navigate through life smoothly.

The truth is... these very same situations haunt us every day because we have not dealt with them. We are not at peace. We tend to carry them along in our everyday life and allow it to generate feelings of anger, rage, defeat, hurt, and pain. It's important that we identify the root of our issues that continually stop us from truly succeeding in life.

When a problem occurs, it is highly likely to be a result of something that is not right with the way you're living. Everything in life has a cause and effect to it. You are in hefty debt, because you didn't live within your means; you got involved in toxic friendships or relationships, because you were too trusting or did not allow yourself to really get to know a person and the list goes on.

Think of your issues like the layers of an onion. When you cut it open each layer is a different size. Well, when it comes to your problems, each issue has a different depth. The objective is to dig as deep as you can to the root of the issue, and then create an action plan on how to heal from that issue. As healing is achieved, you will be launched step by step towards living a happy and healthy life.

In this book, I want to share with you some eye-opening experiences from my journey and self-help methods that have helped me unleash the layers of my bondage. It is my desire to lead you into dissecting these areas and unleash whatever is hindering you from living your life as the best version of you possible.

"There is no one way to recover and heal from any trauma. Each survivor chooses their own path or stumbles across it."

- Laurie Matthew

Unleashing The Layers of Trauma

I joined my family April 16, 1986 in New Orleans, Louisiana as the youngest of three children. I lived in a nice home on an uptown street called General Taylor. It was in that house that many memories were formed, and lessons were learned.

Though there were definitely times I felt as if I got the "short end of the stick." I thought I had everything others only dreamed of. It wasn't until I ventured outside my home and began looking at the lives of others that I quickly realized just how wrong my perception was. On the outside we appeared to be a loving family. My parents had been married for over thirty years. That alone was something to be proud and beam about. Nevertheless, despite the great times we had, there were many not so great times that truly balanced things out.

We were present among one another, but there was no real bond other than blood and DNA to connect us. See, my mother grew up in a household that lacked affection. As my siblings and I grew up, we experienced the same thing. My mother couldn't give us anything that she never experienced. Of course, as a child I didn't understand that. Not only did we not experience affection, but we also never had open talks, family vacations or anything else of the sort. We never took a family photo and to this day we still don't have any. There were many times where I craved love and affection and it was nowhere to be found.

The love I desired but never received, shaped some of the layers that I have had to unleash from my life. My perception of love was driven by what I thought I didn't have. What I saw in other families do. They had emotive love; the hugs, kisses and smiley happy people in the park love. It took some time for my perception to; however, the older I got, the more I understood that even though she wasn't affectionate, she loved us the best way she knew how. She was strong, a provider, and attentive to each us in her own way and because of it, I LOVE her dearly. She always gave what she could to the best of her ability. She's known for her many jokes, her love of the casino, and the way she doted on her family. Regardless of what I felt she lacked, I could still see the good in her. One thing I knew for sure, she loved my father and took care of him until death did them apart. Her loyalty and dedication, in my mind, made up for some of the lack of affection.

My father was a great man. He was a man of strength who brought an abundance of life and laughter to our family. He was also a man that did not play about his wife and three girls! His unconditional love was always visible. Early on in my teenage years, my life took a drastic turn when my health started to decline.

One day I woke up with aches and pains ripping throughout my body. It was so severe I brought it to my parents' attention. I would complain off and on about the widespread of pain; however, no one had a clue where it stemmed from. Our family had several major medical issues that had been prevalent throughout the generations such as Sickle Cell Anemia, Cystic Fibrosis, Arthritis, Gout, and Lupus. So, it could've been any number of things causing such intense pain.

After waking up unable to walk, being hospitalized and undergoing many tests, I was finally diagnosed with Fibromyalgia. Fibromyalgia is a medical condition characterized by the chronic widespread pain and a heightened pain response to pressure. Some symptoms include tiredness to a degree that normal activities are affected. It is associated with depression, anxiety and posttraumatic stress disorder. The cause is unknown; however, it is believed to involve a combination of genetic and environmental factors. I was devastated! All I could do was ask myself "Is this for real?" I wondered why I was the one chosen to have to deal with this.

From that point on, I had many restless nights where I cried myself to sleep wondering why this condition took over my body. It was preventing me from living my best life. As a young person, you just want to be normal. You want to be able to do the things that all the other kids your age can do. Having a debilitating disease was certainly not normal for a teenager.

A few years later, I was diagnosed with Undifferentiated Connective Tissue Disease. Undifferentiated Connective Tissue Disease is an autoimmune disease that affects the joints and the muscles of the body. This means that the system of the body that is responsible for protecting you from infections is attacking the body itself. It typically affects women between the ages of 40-60 years old, however, here I was a child experiencing the same thing and it was too hard to explain to my peers. For the people I did tell, it became a normal thing for them to respond with, "Girl, you are too young to be having those problems," or "You are beautiful!"

I knew both of those things were very true, but I also knew this was just a part of God's plan for me. He has not and never will give me more than I can handle. Despite my health status, I pushed forward and set my focus on school. I refused to allow my condition to hold me hostage. I was in the 11th grade and planned to enjoy my remaining teenage years. While preparing to take my Leap Test, which would have determined if I was moving forward to 12th grade, I received some devastating news.

One night the phone rang. When I answered it was a nurse from Charity Hospital stating that my father had been shot! She said it was pretty bad and she advised we should get there right away. Though it felt like I was in a dream it was a nightmare come true. I was shocked, frazzled and nervous. I had no clue what was about to take place. Since I was the one who answered the phone, I was going to have to be the one to deliver this awful news to my family. I told my mom and sisters. We quickly dressed and rushed to the hospital.

When we arrived, we were told we had to wait until visiting hours to see him because he was deeply sedated. We watched as they rolled him away on a stretcher. His face was very swollen and full of blood. It was a very emotional moment, so I didn't know how to act. We couldn't imagine who would want to hurt a hardworking, family-oriented man.

We later found out about the incident that two guys came in to rob the place from police and others that were there at the time. They told everyone not to move but someone did, and so they started shooting. When my dad was shot in the face and in the thigh, they dropped their guns and the money. The police still needed assistance with catching the robbers and no one was willing to turn them in or testify against them.

Meanwhile, my father underwent surgery to begin repairing his injuries. The doctors were able to remove the bullet from his thigh, but could not retrieve the one in his face, which caused him the most complications. As a result, they didn't think he'd ever recover fully from it. He was placed in ICU where they began to slowly take him off sedation. He was able to talk with us and let us know what happened. My mom was there from morning to night making sure to never leave his side. The night after we heard him speak, we begged her to go home and get some rest.

Seven days later, my father went into cardiac arrest and stopped breathing. It took the staff over ten minutes to bring him back to life. By the time they revived him it was too late to avoid permanent damage. The lack of oxygen left him in a vegetative state. When we received the disturbing call of this tragedy, it changed our lives forever. My mom, sisters, and I were devastated. In a blink of an eye, the man we adored and admired was gone. They tried to give us hope that he may one day recover, but that hope was short lived. He was able to breathe on his own but would never be able to walk or talk again. This was a hard pill to swallow. I never imagined living a life without my father.

With everything that was going on I was emotionally and mentally overwhelmed. It was expected that I go back to school and perform regularly in class. And if my plate wasn't full enough, this particular year, I needed to prepare to take the Leap test. I couldn't help but to wonder how on earth I was going to pass this test with so much on my mind. And now, my family had the additional responsibility of caring for my father.

We learned how to take care of my father by watching the staff at a nursing home. Then we set everything up in our home like a hospital. He was fed and medicated through tubes and had to be washed and cleaned like an infant. We had to take him back and forth to the hospital when he was ill. It was depressing to watch every day, knowing there was nothing my family or I could do to get the man we loved so dearly back.

As bad as I wanted people to understand what I was feeling and going through, I grew to understand this was my journey, not theirs. It was painful and lonely at times even in the midst of family. However, my circumstances were simply layers that were building to be unleashed. These were experiences that I had to go through. It deepened my relationship with God and my understanding of how to overcome mental and emotional pain. I believe the experience was God's way of preparing me to help others to overcome as well. I created methods of coping to help inspire, encourage, and motivate me to get through my difficult moments. Some of those inspirations that aided me in unleashing my layers of lack, trauma and disappointment were:

The Bible

Yolanda Adams songs
The Battle is the Lords & Never Give Up

Marvin Sapp songs
Never Would Have Made It & My Testimony

Fantasia song
Lose to Win

Jekalyn Carr songs
You Will Win & Stay With Me

Tasha Cobb songs
Gracefully Broken & Fill Me Up

Brian Courtney Wilson song
Increase My Faith

We all have the option of being a victim, but we also have the choice of overcoming and rising above for the greater. As we deal with life, it easy to allow ourselves to be vulnerable and weak. The most powerful thing we can do, is take every situation we're handed and produce the best outcome possible. Don't let what you're faced with define who you are. If we follow this motto, we are controlling our life and not letting it be controlled. Determination derived from pain usually rebirths the most beautiful and successful individuals. They have learned how to endure and thrive from their most trying and traumatic moments. Regardless of what you may be facing, God will be your strength to get you through. No matter what the situation is God has a way of making the impossible possible. If it ever feels as if you aren't going to make it through, my testimony is proof to show you all things are possible.

Between dealing with my health issues and losing my father I could've easily given up. However, I put my trust in God. It was through Him that gave me the ability to push through my trials and make it beyond. He was ever faithful as I grieved, cried out in pain, and sat in self-pity. There were times that I felt no one else could possibly understand what I was going through. Whether I was laying in the hospital bed hoping for peace or sitting by my father's side wishing to hear his laugh again, God was with me.

I want you to know that God is always with you, just like He was with me. Even though you may not understand the why behind what you may be facing, time will reveal that this is just another layer to be unleashed from your life. It may not make sense right now, but the path you're on is designed to not only help yourself, but to also be a living testimony for others. You are living testament of strength and perseverance to show that God is truly able to see you through.

The trauma of being diagnosed with a long-term disease as a teen was life changing. It was enough to deal with all by itself, but then you add on the fact that my father was senselessly shot because he was in the wrong place at the wrong time. This not only changed the course of my life, it affected my entire family. Imagine a family who already struggled to communicate emotions; how difficult would it be for them to express their level of suffering.

Imagine the amount of mental fortitude it took to continue to move forward from day to day as if normal, but with a reminder of the loss of life in the next room attached to beeping machines. Imagine needing a hug or a moment of reprieve from your thoughts or loneliness. Imagine not being able to talk to the only people who could understand, your siblings, but not having the access or the words to connect with them. All of these feelings and thoughts create an emotional bottleneck, which leaves an imprint on your soul. But God, it's not permanent.

You cannot just sweep this kind of tragedy under a rug and act as if it never happened. However, it is exactly what some of us try to do. In this chapter, I want to encourage you to unleash any layers of trauma that you have not dealt with.

Here are some helpful things to consider when sorting through the layers of your own trauma in order to heal from it:

Be Patient with Yourself

You deserve to treat yourself gently and with care. There are going to be moments when you struggle to get through the rough patches and emotion turmoil of recovering after a trauma. Know that struggling doesn't mean you're failing at everything you do. It simply means you're growing and developing a new you. Give yourself time to heal. Don't rush the process. Treat yourself like you would treat someone else working their way through the same thing.

Don't Minimize or Ignore Your Feelings

Get in touch with your emotions. It's ok to feel what you feel. The physical body is a direct reflection of your emotional body, and every day is different. Therefore, it's important that you feel that difference, both physically and emotionally. Avoiding your feelings may hinder your recovery.

Breathe

Breathe when you start to feel overwhelmed or stressed. It will help refresh your mind and re-establish a sense of calmness. As you begin to calm down, your body will fall into a more relaxed state. This allows you to think clearly and rationally about any challenges you're facing.

Develop a Routine

If you're feeling stuck in your life, developing a daily practice can be a huge catalyst toward growth and healing. It can be almost anything as long as it gives you the time and space to let go and reconnect with yourself, each and every day. As well as help ease your stress and anxiety.

Get Support

Your healing journey will require a level of strength you can't do all on your own. In your weakest moments when you don't have the energy to do anything that strengthening will come from your support system. Surround yourself with non-judgmental people who are willing to listen. Attending a support group or finding a therapist are also great ways to assist you in your healing journey. Remember, you are not alone... help is always available, if you allow it.

Questions to assist you with unleashing your layers of trauma:

What are some areas in your life where you've experienced major trauma?

_____

_____

_____

_____

_____

_____

_____

How do you believe this affected you?

_____

_____

_____

_____

_____

Have you healed from your traumatic experience? If not, what are some things that are hindering you?

_____

_____

_____

_____

_____

_____

_____

What were some coping mechanisms you used to help you deal with what you were going through?

_____

_____

_____

_____

_____

_____

How has the trauma you've experienced impacted the relationships of those around you?

_____

_____

_____

_____

_____

_____

_____

Name 3 steps you will take to heal from this trauma starting today.

_____

_____

_____

_____

_____

_____

Any problem, big or small, within a family, always seems to start with bad communication. Someone isn't listening.

- Emma Thompson

Unleashing The Layers of Family

My greatest childhood moments were of being a part of my family that was designed especially for me. My two favorite holidays growing up were Thanksgiving and Christmas because all my family would gather together. The elders would cook delicious New Orleans specialties like gumbo, stuffed bell peppers, stuffed mirlitons, heavenly hash, praline candies and much more. I was fond of the time we invested in each other. I was in love with the closeness we felt even though I knew it would be short lived.

Since both sides of my family seemed to consist of a variety of small clicks, neither of which I fit into, those moments we shared allowed me to feel like less of an outcast among them. The holidays were a time where no one was left out. There may not have been much affection or closeness during the other times of the year, but the holidays were a blessing!

I also thoroughly enjoyed spending time with my

great grandmother and cousins. Grandma Mary Tophia was the one person in my life who always made sure I was okay. She taught me everything I know. The quality time I spent with her seemed to tame the aching pains I felt due to the lack of affection from my mother... affection that was the equivalent to love in my eyes. I didn't realize it then, but I know now that my Grandma Mary was a surrogate for the love and affection that I couldn't get from my mother. Unfortunately, due to her living a long beautiful life, she was also called home to Heaven at 95. I was again torn to pieces but understood it was her time.

Over the last 10 years, my mother's health declined due to a mass on her lungs and emphysema. She discovered the news before we did, but initially chose to keep it to herself as her way of shielding us from more heartache. She held it for as long as she could, but she was right about how we would react. When we finally found out about her illness, the news hit us like a ton of bricks. It was both startling and scary.

Honestly, it goes without saying that the hurt was inevitable. The fear of loss we felt was very reminiscent of our experience with our father. Given my mother's quality of life, we needed to act fast. It left us to digest the news while being thrust into a world wind of continuous clinic and hospital visits. Watching her go through moments of extreme shortage in her oxygen levels and high blood pressure are still difficult.

Living without one parent was hard enough but trying to imagine my life without either of them was overwhelming. The weight of that accompanied by the emotional impact her health had on me felt crippling. To add to the weight, I found myself intensely angry that she didn't stop smoking cigarettes, which only exacerbated her situation. And, I seemed to be more concerned than she was. The more I tried to convey how I felt about it, the more we seemed to disconnect from one another. Talking to her about smoking was getting nowhere and watching her continue to harm herself appeared to be hurting me more than it was affecting her. I felt like I was caught in a vice grip. The more I fought and moved against it, the more pulled and crushed I felt. My heart hurt. As hard as it was, I had to realize I needed to take a step back. You can't want more for a person than they want for themselves.

The same disconnect that resided between my mother and I also dwelled amongst My sisters and I. We struggled to bond with one another, because growing up the foundation was never built. We didn't know how to build a closer relationship with one another. We weren't encouraged to be close. We were three outspoken, smart, genuine and strong individuals. In us, God created uniquely strong, beautiful and dynamic women; however, we weren't taught how to be strong together. I always thought it was a plus to have a big sister. To have someone who would hold my hand as I dealt with tough moments, comfort me during my medical flares, and hug me when I was having a bad day, but that never happened. As trials arose and life happened there was no glue keeping us together.

We looked at life through separate lenses that contained drastically different realities. As much as we all wanted to be close, it always eluded us. It was as if somehow, being connected was a threat to our individuality or our own unique perspectives. Somehow, the desire for a sisterly bond was internally interpreted as being weak or needy. Making room for each other didn't mean letting go of our individuality or our belief in our capabilities as women. Just like with my mother, any expression of concern or care created a needless tug-of-war; it became a battle for autonomy and self-sufficiency. Neither of which was in question or under threat. Our disagreements over the years twisted my trust and were added to some of my first lessons in heartbreak.

It wasn't until I changed my perspective on how things should've been that I was able to let go of the hurt I held on to. One thing we all learned over the years was that we coincided better in our own spaces. I also learned that each of us could have done more to build, maintain and nourish the bond between us. When you love a person it's easier to love your perception of them than it is to love them for who they really are. I had to grow to understand that my sisters were just as broken as I was living life as if we were whole. They had and have their own set of trials and tribulations they've had to endure. Today, we talk more and we're planning a sister's trip together, but it definitely was a process getting here.

I'm working toward letting go of my own desires for a specific type of relationship with my siblings. I am beginning to understand that what I wanted may flourish over time. We are going to have to work harder to build a bone with one another. Hopefully we can have the necessary conversations to begin the process of unleashing the layers of family rejection and denial. More importantly, as we heal from the past, we can accept each other as we are and where we are.

The trials I've faced in my life impacted me down to my core, but fighting my way through to find my own emotional healing was the greatest reward of all. Through it all I came to the realization that it was time to let go, so that I could grow. You are not in charge of controlling the outcomes in your life, but you have full control over you.

Part of my process was to also let go of my mother. The frustrations I held towards her were keeping me stuck in in a state of resentment. I had to grow to understand that letting go didn't mean I loved her any less or stopped wanting the best for her. What she continued to do to bring her health down was still bothersome and I didn't want anything bad to happen to her. It just meant that I would have to remember that she is fully aware of her decisions; she is an adult and in fact my mother. It wasn't the other way around. My opinions and well intentions were neither requested nor desired.

So, while I was not okay with the idea of losing her to a completely preventable situation, what I had control over was my ability to release it all to a higher power. God was greater than my frustration. And He was going to have to handle this His way. I could not live her life for her. And I could not let this control my mind, thoughts and peace any longer. I had to unleash the layer of feeling guilty, because I loved her more than she showed that she loved herself. I had to unleash the pain of me never getting what I desired from her, because it was keeping me in bondage and not allowing me to fulfill my duty as a mother.

I think I was still hoping that my mother would love me enough to do something different than she had ever done before. Even though it was unlikely, I wanted it. But, when my desire for my mother started to affect the way I related to my own children, I knew I had to let her go. I was so stuck in what I wanted from her after all these years, my desire overshadowed my reason. My anger would bleed over into my day or the next activity after leaving my mother's side.

After hospital visits, I was literally checked out, consumed in my feelings. I found myself always trying to navigate a myriad of emotions; resentment always at the top of the list, disappointment a close second. I didn't realize how much time it was taking away from my life, my children, and my own goals as a parent. It is interesting how we try so hard not to be the things we resented growing up. Yet, here I am headstrong, determined to take care of everyone and everything, and neglecting to shower my own babies with affection.

The difference between my mother and I was that I knew better. I knew I had to be intentional about prioritizing a need over a want. I wanted my mother to do better, but I needed my children to know without a doubt I loved them, in thought, word, and deed. I needed to unleash my expectations of her, those unrealistic and warranted. She did the best she could and I was now in position to do even better than she. God-willing.

I had to learn that there's no such thing as a perfect family. I had to unleash my layer of bondage, pain, and resentment and welcome in peace, patience, unconditional love, and wisdom. I prayed over myself and my family daily but ultimately, I knew God had the final say. Building a solid foundation where there is none is all in the effort you put into it. You have to make it a point to continue loving a person beyond the issues you have with them.

When I shifted my focus and changed my perspective, God was able to rebuild me in a way I couldn't do on my own. I was able to see myself in this situation from a different perspective. Sometimes the focus you put on others is what you really need for yourself. When I was able to redirect my attentiveness towards the areas in my life I felt I lacked, in this case the affection and love from my mother, I was able to begin healing the process. God even placed people in my life that gave me some of the things I felt like I was missing. It was like they were strategically placed to show me and then grow me to be a better me. These people are some of my closest friends who welcomed me in and loved me unconditionally. I am forever grateful for each of them.

As family you are not going to get along 100% of the time. Nor are you going to agree on everything. There are too many personalities, too many mindsets, and too many variables that guarantee that fact. Nevertheless, when disagreements do arise you have to be willing to get to the root of what caused the issues to begin with. Really take a deep look into your stance. Consider the reason you feel the way you feel. Is it because of the situation or did the situation trigger a memory from an earlier experience? Sometimes our reactions to things have absolutely nothing to do with the situation at hand, but instead are behavioral imprints from our past experiences.

For example, because I wasn't close to my siblings and had been taken advantage of too many times, I felt like an outcast. I had gotten so accustomed to it that it turned into indifference towards building close relationships. I automatically assumed that posture in different social circles and relationships. When people tried to get close to me, I rejected them before they could me. When they would try to address my behavior towards them, I would be dismissive or indignant towards them. In my mind, I was protecting myself and my space from further rejection and abuse.

What I didn't realize was that I had created an impenetrable wall. Anyone who tried to cross over was subject to my projection of pain. How they responded in turn validated my decision to keep them at arm's length. This projection was on autopilot to be employed in any situation. And with certain people, to include my family, this cycle caused a lot of animosity and many a disagreement. It has to be said...you can't move forward from an issue until you get to the root of the problem and deal with the negative feelings it caused. It requires a great deal of patience and even more transparency.

Now, step into the other person's shoes in an effort to understand why they acted the way they did. Have you truly listened from their point of view or were you only interested maintaining yours? Take a step back and take a look at yourself. What role did you play in the situation? Was there a chance that you misinterpreted what was said? Is it possible that you were wrong or could have handled things differently? Many times, we act out of our emotions, which enhance an already festering situation. When you were able to calm down, did you consider how your words may have added fuel to the disagreement? What we should really do is take a step back and take your hands off the situation until you can think clearly and rationally.

Be willing to take responsibility for your actions and the role you played in the situation. Then apologize. We don't always want to be the bigger person, but sometimes it's necessary in order to maintain our peace. Sometimes it's necessary because it's the right thing to do. We are ultimately responsible for our words and actions. We are responsible for the seeds we place in the hearts of the people we are in relationships with. It is true, we reap what we sow. You truly have to be willing to lay your aughts and pride down, to find your path to reconciliation. It's not about right or wrong, or who did what when or why? What was the objective of the conversation in the first place? Was it to be heard or to bridge a gap? Was it a roundabout way to elicit a show of love or acceptance? A lot of disagreements can be resolved if you simply make an effort to understand things from the other person's perspective.

Please don't hold a grudge towards someone you love. It's toxic and doesn't allow for the hope of it to ever be resolved. The only thing it does is solidify your role as a victim of past wrongs. Your pain and suffering becomes your identity. Meanwhile, it isolates the person you love and your heart from reconciliation. What about today? Is what happened then prolific enough to impact a healthy loving relationship today? Was the disagreement more than the sum of the goodness of the relationship?

It's ok to disagree but be willing to make amends after falling out. Life is too short for grudges. Remember, your loved ones could be here today and gone tomorrow. Forgive them and move forward. However, if whatever took place between you is an unforgivable act, then deal with them with accordingly; with a long-handled spoon; this means you need to set boundaries or remove yourself entirely in order to protect your peace.

In order to unleash the layers in this section, I want you to think of some family situations that you have been affected by in the past. Be honest about what happened and think about how it could have been handled better. It's ok to look at what other people did, but you also have to be willing to admit to own shortcomings. This is not to place blame or cause shame. This is designed to help you figure this out so that you do not have to repeat the same cycle again.

Here are some helpful things to consider when working towards overcoming family issues:

Establish Family Time

Family time ensures that strong family bonds are developed. Set aside time to have quality family discussions to share good news, plans, and issues that may be brewing. You'd be surprised that it helps build good self-esteem in your children and reinforces positive behaviors. Most importantly, quality family time allows you to reconnect and create beautiful memories.

Try To Resolve Conflict

Stay focused on the current issue. It is easy to get caught up in the emotions of shame, guilt, distractions and the blame game. By addressing the problem and not the person, you have a better chance of minimizing hostility and finding resolution. It is essential to stay transparent, an active listener and respectful to every perspective. Above all give everyone the benefit of the doubt that they too are invested resolving conflict.

Acknowledge and Validate

Acknowledging family members makes everyone feel understood and validated. The byproduct is appreciation, respect, and better self-esteem. Acknowledgement is an intentional form of affirmation that encourages a spirit of gratitude. Because, emotions can run high in family discussions, how you express yourself matters. The benefit of validation is that it communicates that each person is important and what they think and feel has value. Validating each person's point of view ensures that each person contributes in empathy, selflessness and the spirit of collaboration.

Look For the Common Ground

Find ways to bring clarity to a situation by establishing ground rules to finding a solution. Since a family problem involves everyone, everyone has to participate in brainstorming a peaceable solution. Allow for positive and negative input and encourage reaching a solution as a team. Compromise is always the name of the game but do so in truth and in agreement from all parties.

Apologize

An apology goes a long way. It disarms, allows people to remain connected and repairs relationships. It also removes unnecessary stress, shame and guilt and jump starts conversation again. Apologies helps us to get unstuck from past hurts and moves us into a space where healing is possible. The incredible part is that an apology humanizes you; it asserts your humility and vulnerability and diminishes your image as the enemy, opposition or the person who wronged another. You're no longer viewed through the lens of anger or resentment, but forgiveness. Even if you don't feel as if did anything wrong, apologizing will do much to establish empathy and compassion. It will also set the grounds for forgiveness and reconciliation. Seek first to resolve conflicts and heal. And always be sincere.

Forgive

Forgiveness frees you from the hostility of the past. It does not mean you condone what happened, but it does alleviate you from being stuck in victimization and resentment. Forgiveness lays aside pride and removes the barriers resentment, bitterness and anger. It also allows for compassion to present itself to begin the process of healing hurts. A hardened heart pushes people away and denies you of the love you deserve, so forgive. Forgive to unlock the best in everyone, especially you.

Questions to assist you with unleashing your layers:

How did your actions affect the situation at hand?

_____

_____

_____

_____

_____

_____

_____

_____

Could things have been communicated differently to defuse the situation?

What could you have done differently to resolve the situation?

_____

_____

_____

What has helped you deal with similar issues in the past?

_____

_____

_____

_____

_____

_____

Sometimes talking to someone who has dealt with a similar experience helps. Do you know of others who have experienced these types of problems who you can talk with?

_____

_____

How will you face challenges the next time it arises?

Thinking back over your own family feuds what are something you may have misunderstood, or could I be getting wrong?

Layers Unleashed

_____

_____

_____

_____

Life is about trusting your feelings and taking chances, losing and finding happiness, appreciating the memories, learning from the past, and realizing people change.

- Atul Purohit

Unleashing The Layers of Marriage

Since my father was taken from me at such a critical time in my life, I didn't have a male figure to coach me on the rights and wrongs of dating from a man's perspective. I longed for him at pivotal life markers where his guidance probably would have deterred me from some of the decisions I made. He would never have the opportunity to see me graduate from high school or college. He never got to screen or threaten the lives of the young men I dared to bring home. He would never wipe the tears from my face from certain heartbreak. He certainly never had the privilege of walking me down the aisle to say I do. These are all very hard moments to think about even now.

I missed him then, I miss him now. Even now, 13 years later it's still hard to accept my life without him in it. However, instead of dwelling on it, I now choose to take with me as many pieces of him as I can. What do

I mean? Well one of the things I admired most about my father was his love and commitment in his marriage. He was dedicated to loving and upholding my mother beyond what I've seen in most marriages even today. As a result, my mother and father were married for years. Their love and dedication to each other set the standard for what I desired to have for myself.

In meeting my Husband, he definitely embodied some of my Father's best qualities. He is a strong family man who believes in taking care of his family's needs. He is a man of very few words, but his love shines through his provision and attentiveness; making sure every necessity is met. After dating several Mr. Wrongs, God sent me a breath of fresh air; someone who was a man of his word through action. We've now been married for 3 years. Marriage is a continuous learning process that helps us learn to compromise with, compliment, and complete one another better. Our bond grows stronger through the process as we work toward gaining understanding and patience with one another.

Peeling back the layers of my hurt and pain to be able to love and trust again wasn't easy, but it was well worth it. His strength and endurance gave me the push I needed to complete the work unleashing these layers. We continue to build a foundation that we both desire and work hard at, in the good and bad times. I look forward to celebrating our life for many more years to come. Believe me when I tell you bliss doesn't happen overnight. It is detrimental to pretend and set that expectation for yourself, especially early in the marriage. The good thing is that the honeymoon phase is very real and wonderful. But the struggle is real. You have to adapt to each other — blend lives, furniture and sometime even children.

If you were blessed with having a long engagement and transparent communication, you would know each other's habits, pet peeves, maturity level with bills and cleanliness, external relationships, and personal goals. It takes time to find solid ground with each while going through this process. It's unsettling and uncomfortable going through the transition from me to us. We are new to this, so we have plenty of work left to do. They say anything worth having is worth fighting for and marriage definitely is worth the fight. I love my husband to life and I absolutely cherish what we have. I've heard it said it gets better after year 5. Well, we are already successfully on our way to marriage bliss.

Had I continued playing the dozens with the "what-ifs and maybe's", the relationship I have with my husband would be non-existent. Those types of scenarios without a solution will not set you up to be successful. However, having a plan in place with contingencies, accounting for those "what-ifs and maybe's," will guarantee movement in the right direction and possibly the right mate. Try to accommodate everything you have in mind that will better your life and help you get closer to your end goal.

Your dreams are worth digging into. Although, there may be some challenges, obstacles and possibly even setbacks, the only way to find out is to put your all into your plan and goals. As you set a goal, start taking small steps, making sure that you learn the lessons and account for the details that shape your relationship towards success. Trying to hit the end goal right from the start, will guarantee a repeat in lessons sometime down the line. Take your time and learn to enjoy journey that marriage brings.

There are some people who have success right away in their marriage. You know who they are. They are living the dream: two beautiful professionals who were best friends before they fell in love create the dream wedding and a fantasy honeymoon. They come back home to a gorgeous mini mansion. Oh, and they have successful careers and eventually have 2.5 absolutely adorable children. They are perfect. We should all be so blessed. However, you should never judge or compare someone else's success to yours. You should also never get discouraged, because you think you should have the same successes as someone else.

Remember your plan and goals are just as beautiful and are tailored just for you. If you are constantly looking at what someone else is doing, that means the time you're invested in sowing into jealousy is taking away from you sowing into the success and strength of your own plan. Every system and process comes with trial, error and growth. Those who fail are those who never try or go back to the endless cycle of "what ifs and maybes." We are not perfect, and we have to allow ourselves to make mistakes.

It's how you persevere is what helps you grow. How you endure humility and setbacks is what defines you as a person and a couple. Through God all things are possible and there is nothing to bigger or greater than Him. If you have fallen or detoured off your plan, this does not mean you have failed, it means you needed to learn a lesson via the scenic route. It will take just a little longer, but it's ok and so are you. Get up and go with God. And believe with your whole heart that you will have what he promised you and all that you can think, ask or imagine. God bless your union.

According to the American Psychological Association 40-50% of married couples in the United States end in divorce. Despite such a high percentage, let me be the first to tell you that marriage is a blessing. It has its highs and lows, wow moments and challenges, so one should never be under the impression or enter into marriage expecting a fairytale. The biggest thing to realize is that your mate is only human. They are flawed, scarred, and still growing as are you. And it will take accepting those flaws, and healing those scars through love and patience, that will allow you to grow together. Events will occur good and bad that will allow you to really get to know your spouse. Often times we get upset or fall in disagreements, because of a lack of communication. We sometimes are disabled by not fully being able to understand what your spouse needs, want or how they feel. The biggest thing is patience and not assuming the other person is a mind reader.

Encourage each other and be one another's biggest supporters in good and bad moments. Be willing to table a disagreement in order to allow space and peace to bring clarity. Sometimes a little space is good to let one another think about the situation at hand before tackling it. Always be vigilant in remembering, it's not about right or wrong, but God and love. Err on the side of unity and the better good for all. Be on one accord with the household such as major decisions with children and finances. A good and enduring marriage thrives because of times where forgiveness covered a multitude of sins, especially for hurtful things said or done... It takes two good forgivers to enjoy many years together.

What kind of love do you feel when you look at your partner? Is it adoration and appreciation? Be sure to brighten your spouse's day with sweet and kind words. Take time to date each other. Court each other like you did in the beginning. Share new insights and perspectives you learned with your spouse. That means to stay talking, stay interested in what makes your spouse's brain ticking and heart happy. Stay encouraged through the thick and then. And most importantly, in everything you do turn and talk to God and ask him for his guidance.

Keep in mind not all issues are relevant ones. Take a moment to think about what issues are most important to you. Be honest and transparent with one another about your feelings. A lot more can be resolved speaking freely and honestly than holding things inside. Ask yourself are there any past conflicts we should resolve? It's hard to move forward if there are unresolved conflicts. Not only will the past keep coming up in future arguments, but it's hard to get close to someone if you are still angry about something they said or did. If there is a specific source of contention, identify when it originated. Determine whether if it is the actual issue that occurred that offends you or if it is how you felt when it occurred that is the true pain point.

Also, consider whether new disagreements or arguments that happen that bring up similar feelings is the trigger that brings up those old issues. If the answer is yes, then it is important that you recognize the triggers and resolve within yourself why you are still holding onto that pain. If you need to forgive your spouse, then do so wholly. Apologize for any offense you may have cause while operating with the lens of unforgiveness on. Don't forget to forgive yourself.

In the spirit of reconciliation, always do a self-check. Search your heart for areas that need attention, so that you won't punish or project onto your spouse. Your marriage depends on your ability to forgive, extend grace, and express empathy and compassion. If there are any unresolved issues, take time to discuss and create strategies for working on them together. You can only grow stronger in unity and the covenant of marriage.

One of the most important aspects of a relationship is communication. You have to be vigilant to keep the lines of communication open. Hurt feelings tend to throw up barriers and the first thing to suffer is your ability to communicate. Remember, that your spouse is your covering; they are responsible for hearing your heart and they cannot do that if your communication is hindered. In Matthew 15:18 (KJV) it says, "But those things which proceed out of the mouth come forth from the heart; and they defile the man." This means what you say to your spouse communicates the condition of your heart.

Yes, if you are hurt you are more likely to say harsh things; however, be mindful that what leaves your mouth may also leave an imprint on your spouse's heart that may also take some time to repair. Speak truthfully, but in grace with a spirit of unity and love. If you can't talk to one another comfortably, you will never be able to work through future problems. Find new ways to improve communication with one another without judging or getting angry.

Here are some helpful things to consider when developing and maintaining a healthy marital relationship.

Build Togetherness

Establish a solid foundation with one another by building togetherness. By doing so you are in turn building an understanding and a solid foundation of communication between the two of you. At the same time set boundaries to protect and respect each other's space and feelings.

Value and Protect Your Relationship

Build a bond that consists of love, understanding, respect and all other positive factors. If these traits are present in a relationship, nobody would tell you to value your relationship. Also, if you have a relationship you value so much, you would do everything possible to make it work. Learn to continue the work of protecting the privacy of you and your spouse as a couple. Discuss problems with one another before going to an outside source.

Be a Safe Haven for Your Spouse

Maintain the strength of the marital bond in the face of adversity. The marriage should be a safe haven in which partners are able to express their differences, anger and conflict. Discuss problems as they arise. Don't allow negative feelings to fester.

Keep It Light

The world can be a tough place so make your home a place of relief and relaxation. A place where neither you nor your spouse can wait to get to. Use humor and laughter to keep things in perspective and to avoid boredom and isolation. Never stop dating one another so the spark between you will never go out.

Show Your Love

The love in a relationship continues to grow from strength to strength, and it isn't just the love that grows, so many other positive factors grow along with it, with this the relationship is sure of longevity. Relationships are better off when couples aren't just lovers but are friends as well. Passion comes naturally; doing things regularly with your partner stimulates certain feeling and emotions, and those feelings and emotions are what make passion grow. Nurture and comfort each other.

Show Your Appreciation

There are times when couples become so familiar with each other that the marriage starts to feel like a routine. Remind your spouse that you appreciate them by saying thank you for the little things. Be supportive of their goals and dreams by offering continuous encouragement and support.

Communicate, Communicate, and Communicate

I can't stress to you enough the importance of developing a strong level of communication with one another. Not communicating properly with your spouse can kill your relationship. If you feel like you and your spouse are no longer connecting with each other like you used to, say something right away and work toward improving it. Be sure to be honest and transparent no matter what the situation is.

Watch Your Words

Words are powerful weapons that can shape the essence of the way a person feel about themselves. In a marriage don't say things to intentionally hurt your spouse. Constant negativity towards a person will cause them to shut down and eventually want out of the relationship. Think about what you really mean to say and then say that instead. Be kind and encouraging with your words.

Maintain Intimacy

Keep the intimacy and passion alive in your relationship both inside and outside the bedroom. Don't let others define what is considered "normal" or "healthy" in your marriage. Know that just because you may do things different in your marriage from someone else doesn't have your relationship is any less exciting or fun. Intimacy and passion comes in many shapes and forms, including conversation and cuddling.

Questions to assist you with unleashing your layers:

Do you feel you and your partner clearly communicate with one another?

_____

_____

_____

_____

_____

_____

_____

_____

Are you positively affecting each other's life?

_____

_____

_____

_____

_____

_____

_____

Laughter is good for the soul. How often do you laugh together?

_____

_____

_____

_____

_____

_____

_____

Do you spend time dating your partner?

_____
_____
_____
_____
_____
_____
_____

How do you show your love for each other?

_____
_____
_____
_____
_____
_____
_____

Do you bring up arguments very often and why?

_____

_____

_____

_____

_____

_____

_____

Have you ever apologized for what you've done wrong to your partner?

_____

_____

_____

_____

_____

_____

Do you forgive your partner's mistakes easily?

_____

_____

_____

_____

_____

_____

Do you throw temper easily for small mistakes of your partners?

_____

_____

_____

_____

_____

_____

_____

Do you look forward to your future with your partner?

_____

_____

_____

_____

_____

_____

_____

Do you respect each other?

_____

_____

_____

_____

_____

_____

_____

Have you seen each other at your best and worst?

_____

_____

_____

_____

_____

_____

_____

> "Don't make money your goal. Instead, pursue the things you love doing, and then do them so well that people can't take their eyes off you."
>
> - Maya Angelou

Unleashing The Layers of Finances

RIDING AROUND AND GETTING IT.... At one time this was definitely a popular song for me by 2 Chains. I remember many others and myself riding around jamming this song. I'm not going to lie... it sounded good, the beat was banging, and the lyrics were fly. In that moment, I thought it was true. The reality of it is that so many of us use these songs as our anthems to hype us up and make us feel good. When, in actuality, we were far from riding around and getting anything! Let's just consider it positive affirmation.

There were many days I had no clue how I was going to eat, where I was going to sleep, how I was going to survive or where my life was headed next. I wasn't riding around getting anything but air and a dream. By the time things turned around financially I began mishandling my money. It's funny how you make all these plans for what you're going to do when you finally arrive. But, when the opportunity comes around the only thing you do is try to make up for all the time you did not have money. Money is called currency for a reason. Similar to running rivers, it flows in the direction of lower altitude. That means it either seeps in to the ground or into other bodies. Well my money refused to stay in my purse, falling instead into stores, people or other wasteful ventures.

Children have a tendency to inherit some of our parents' bad habits. I mentioned some of the bad times in my household growing up. In our home it was gambling. My parents were either gambling or partying and as a result they struggled to make ends meet. While I had good memories of my parents laughing, dancing and carrying on, there were various things I desired to do like modeling or joining a girl's singing group that were overlooked due to financial issues.

Unfortunately, instead of going in the opposite direction of my parents, I imitated them. Before I could even turn 21, I had already turned into a huge gambler myself. By 2013 I had spent over $40k! Gambling was a part of me. When you grow up around certain behaviors, you don't think anything is wrong with it. Cursing, smoking, and in my case gambling was a way of life. It's just what we did. I knew I needed to change in order to get better.

But, how? That's what I saw growing up. Everyone around me was doing it. It's very difficult to put down an addictive behavior when it's your normal. I saw and experienced the negative effects of my habit, but because my perception was skewed into believing there was nothing wrong with it, my life started to fall apart. Though I learned from my parents, I had no one to blame but myself.

Breaking habits don't happen overnight, and I needed something transformative. Breaking the bonds of addiction took time as well as consistent effort. Every 12-step program starts with the same mantra: the first step in making a change is admitting you have a problem. Ok, I had a problem. I needed restoration in a way that would propel me to a new way of thinking. Then I had to take action against it. My first action was to decide that I wanted something different.

This way was not working. I prayed that God would strengthen me and provide me with the clarity, insight and help I needed to defeat this addiction. I knew this meant some really big life changes. Though I had some trepidation, I was ready. Truth is with any addiction you may have to get away from the people and places you are used to. You may have to be willing to take on a new normal. From personal experience, it is worth it. God promised an abundant life and the decisions I made up to this point was preventing it. I desired and deserved to live abundantly, but I needed to do the work, as will you.

Now this next step will take every bit of personal integrity and honesty for you to do. You have to take an inventory of your financial situation. You may not have a gambling problem like I did; however, you can look at these next questions from your own perspective:

- What unnecessary things are you spending money on?

- Better yet, what habits do you have that are taking away from your income?

- Do you use money to gamble that you need to pay debts or resolve other financial obligations?

- Do you gamble to escape reality, worry or issues?

- Are you robbing Peter to pay Paul?

- Is your money funny and your change a little strange?

- In all seriousness, are you struggling to live paycheck to paycheck?

- Have you ever thought to harm yourself to escape your problem?

As you gain a better understanding of yourself and healthier financial concepts, you can begin the process of getting back on track. With all the things you'll need to establish a plan to fix the issues at hand. Are you wondering why you have to go through so much just to get started? Well, it's because you can't fix something without knowing what you're fixing or why you're fixing it. And, you're worth it.

Now that you've gotten all of that out of the way, let's proceed. First, make a list of your needs verses your wants. For clarity, let's define the difference between a need and a want. From an economical perspective, a need is something you absolutely have to have in order to survive; you cannot live without it. A want is simply a desire or something that would upgrade your current situation, mood or make your life better in your opinion. In short, a need is something you have to have; a want is something you'd like to have. This doesn't work unless you're honest with yourself. Making excuses or trying to validate your poor choices, negates any work or effort you've done thus far.

When reviewing your list, do you find yourself spending more money on your wants than your needs? If so, that means your way of thinking is broken and you need to be reprogrammed. And that's ok! It is possible to turn things around financially. Rebooting your mindset to prioritize a better quality of life will make room for the things you wish to have. For instance, one way of doing that is by paying your bills first, then only using cash for your purchases. If you don't have enough cash, you can't do whatever it is you're trying to do. You'll find that you will automatically make different and wiser choices knowing you have minimized resources on hand.

One way to start rebooting your mindset is by evaluating and examining each purchase prior to making it. If you are low on money, ask yourself is this item a necessity? If it's not, classify it as a want or a desire and plan for it verse spontaneously spending money you may need later. You can also ask yourself things such as

- How long will the item last?
- Can this wait?

- Do I really need it now?
- Can I find this cheaper somewhere else?
- Will I regret buying this later

As you consistently go through these questions, you're conditioning yourself to think differently about your spending habits.

Credit cards tend to be another issue that aids in horrible spending habits. They make it too easy to develop a dismissive mindset regarding spending money. It could also be said the motion of swiping a credit card might be as addictive as the hand to mouth motion for eating or smoking cigarettes, thus the term "shopaholic". On a positive note, you have more bargaining ability with cash. Knowing you only have so much cash to work with will make you a shrewd negotiator and more attentive to sales and savings comparisons. If you are in debt from the misusing credit cards... stop using it. Cut up your credit cards so you won't be tempted to use them.

Create a budget and stick to it. Your budget is simply your plan for how to make your money work for you. Review your expenses and closely track your spending habits. To some degree, your 'needs versus wants' assessment points a finger at some of your habits. When you track your spending, you'll be better equipped to identify specific frequent expenditures. Some things are so much a part of our day; we don't notice that it happens. For example, do you always stop at a certain gas station and pick up a cup of coffee and a hot cinnamon roll? How often do you go to certain stores? When you get a good grasp of where your money is going, you are ready to set a few financial goals. So in the spirit of excellence, you'll need to do the following:

Calculate Your Expenses

Review all of your receipts, bank statements and any other financial documents. Add all of your expenditures for the last 12 months and no less than 6 months and then divide by the number of months that you can responsibly account for. Do not forget to account for unexpected situations, like a broken air condition or a bad tire. You should have an average monthly expense from this formula.

Figure Out Your Actual Income

Calculate your salary and any additional money you make. Even include your side hustle funds. If you collect alimony or child support, add that to your income. If you pay either of those, delete it from your income.

Set Savings and Debt Relief Goals

This may be painful for you; however, it must be done: Be prepared to eliminate or reduce frivolous expenses. A mocha latte every day from your favorite coffee shop can be an expensive habit. The average American spends approximately $1,100 a year on coffee. Imagine what you could do with that. It's not that you can't have coffee anymore; you'll only need to rely on more practical ways to get coffee, such as make it yourself. Apply this thinking to other items eliminated from your expenses. Calculate how much you can really put toward those goals after covering your basic living expenses. Once you have your monthly budget, subtract 10% of that and put it in your savings. This 10% is to never, ever be touched.

Practice saving money on a regular basis. This includes those who are in debt. Even if it is only $5 a month, develop a discipline of saving. Save a small amount on a regular basis no matter what it is. Now, you realistically determine what your savings goals will be. Set a financial goal to work towards. There's nothing more inspiring than setting a goal and reaching it. The feeling you get from it will encourage you to keep going. Start off with something small and easily attainable.

For example, set a goal to save $50.00 until your next pay period. Once you've succeeded repeat it again. By the following pay period you've already reached $100.00. Continue building on this. As you continue to set and reach your goals, you'll become more aware of your income and your spending habits. Before long you'll notice things you used to desire, you won't want to do anymore. It's totally ok to celebrate your financial wins. Remember, money isn't your enemy. Spending when you don't have money is!

As you are getting a grip on your finances you also want to set small amounts of money aside to invest. Investing is essential to good money management because it ensures both your present and future financial security. Not only do you end up with more money in the bank, but you also end up with another income stream. Investing is the only way to achieve both growing wealth and passive income. If you are a beginner in this part of the financial stability process, there are several investment and budgeting apps that can help manage your money. A few are listed below:

- Albert
    - This app aids saving up for a rainy day, budgeting, tackling debt, investing, and prepare for retirement.
- Joy - Money App
    - This app acts as a money coach for you. It rates your purchases and helps you save money.
- Chime
    - This is a mobile banking app that will help you stay in control of your money and track your spending.
- Mint: Personal Finance & Money
    - This is a free money management and financial tracker that helps you get ahead and stay ahead.
- Cash Account
    - Opening a savings account and having a certain amount go from your checking into that savings account is also a great way to get you started saving. This account should act as

your rainy day fund. It should only be available to you in emergency situations.

It's not how much you earn; it's what you do with what you've earned

- Disclaimer: Keep in mind you might not see profits immediately

- Remember to always pay yourself first

- Keep track of what's coming in, and what's going out. (Monthly)

- Live a minimalistic life to achieve wealth sooner

Sometimes a good pep talk with yourself can really get you fired up! Take a look in the mirror and have a coming to Jesus moment with yourself. Know that it is time that you make a commitment that no matter what and you will use **only** what you need. No, you will not overspend or buy things that have no urgent need in your life. Now is the time that you take total control of your finances. Money doesn't own you, you own money!

Better yet, being a good steward over your finances releases more opportunity to have a better quality life. Though it is not specifically directed towards finances, the concept of stewardship is referenced in the Bible. In Matthew 25:21 it says, His master said to him, 'Well done, good and faithful servant. You have been faithful over a little; I will set you over much. Enter into the joy of your master.' Align yourself accordingly.

Money is a means, not an end. It's a tool you use to reach your goals, whether that goal is to save for an emergency or get out of debt. Learning to get your financial life on track is simply learning to use that tool properly. Change the way you view the money. It's less about being good with money and more about learning to use it to accomplish what matters to you most. Most of personal finance is about mindset, and a simple shift in thinking can make all the difference.

Here are some financial affirmations to keep you motivated and encouraged along the way:

- I move from poverty thinking to prosperity thinking and my finances reflect this change.
- I am a money magnet.
- I am debt free. Money is constantly flowing into my life.
- I walk in abundance all my needs are met.
- My money makes money.
- My money consciousness is always increasing and keeping me surrounded by money.
- I am a good steward over my blessings.
- I control my money; my money does not control me.
- I create wealth and live rich in faith, love and family.

- I walk in my purpose. Peace, healthy, and wealth with follow.

- Every day I am attracting and saving more and more money.

Questions to assist you with unleashing your layers:

What have you decided to let go of in order to grow financially?

_____

_____

_____

_____

_____

_____

_____

_____

_____

_____

Do you monitor your spending habits?

_____

_____

_____

_____

_____

_____

_____

Do you have an accountability partner to keep you on track with your budget?

_____

_____

_____

_____

_____

_____

_____

What are 3 of your financial goals?

_____

_____

_____

_____

_____

_____

What steps are you taking to achieve them?

_____

_____

_____

_____

_____

_____

_____

What skills can I add to my life that will decrease the amount of money I spend but still allow me to enjoy my life?

_____

_____

_____

_____

_____

_____

_____

_____

_____

"A friend is someone who understands your past, believes in your future, and accepts you just the way you are."

– Unknown

Unleashing The Layers of Friendships

Friendship is a close association between two people marked by feelings of care, respect, admiration, concern, and love. Maintaining a friendship is just like maintaining any other relationship. It takes work! It will have its ups and downs, but the good should outweigh the bad.

Life is not great all the time. I've had my fair share of bad friendships, but they helped me to define the type of friend I truly wanted. I desire friends who are real, transparent, genuine and are open in sharing that they have real issues. I want the type of friendship that will allow me to be able to walk with you through your trials and tribulations, just like I would want you to walk with me through mine. I need to know that I'm loved, supported and truly accepted flaws and all. And, I don't expect for my friends to always agree with me.

As a matter of fact, I want them to tell me when I'm out of order or when I could do or handle things better. What I do not want is someone who pretends. I don't want to have to figure out the mask for the day. If you are angry, in pain or resentful, please share that. If you are struggling or just in a mood, let me be there to support and encourage you. I have experienced a great deal in my short life and my desire is to help someone come out of where I came from. If there is any wisdom or life lessons I can share to prevent anyone from going through what I went through, I want my friends to be the automatic beneficiaries of that wisdom.

A true friend will be there with you through the good and the bad. They are not just in it for times of abundance when everything is going well in your life. Friendships require a certain amount of loyalty and consistency. When I am at my worst you will cry with me and then lift me up until I get back to my mountain top and I will reciprocate when you need me. There is no valley too deep where I won't come to get you. A true testament of friendship is that they become your family.

Some people are needy of friends, because they are afraid of being alone. Desperate to be heard, understood or loved will keep some people stuck in a vicious cycle of depending on anyone to satisfy that need. They are willing to risk all of their personal business for a listening ear. This leaves them open to gossipers that thrive on drama and have no problem running to tell their business. The pain and suffering they endure is entertainment for some people, but because of the attention they get, they are blind to the truth. I pray that the love of God heals people desperate for this type of attention. Each time they endure the disappointment of getting hurt, they end up more fragmented and even more damaged.

Some people are in obligated friendships, sort of like a contract. If you entertain the tearing down of people, gossiping or spreading lies, you tend to hang with people that are similar. Like they say, "birds of a feather, flock together." That old adage is so very true. Though it may not be true in every situation, it could be easily assumed that if your "associates" have a certain reputation, then you may also. These types of people usually are afraid to walk away. I realized a long time ago that what people are willing to do to others, no matter how close you think you maybe you are not exempt from receiving that same treatment. Neither I nor you should ever want a friend that bad.

It's safe to give an associate a 90-day trial but after that let it go. If the friendship is not genuine, if it's not drama free...let it go! A real friend should be there through your good and bad moments, they should be able to have adult conversations when they may have hurt the others feelings. Fake friends walk away; real friends know what this looks like. Know when you have met a genuine friend. Everyone you meet does not belong in that category. It's ok to have associates. These are people that you are cordial to, may share a meal with or attend a function with. However, this is not a person that you would share your most intimate thoughts and feelings with. Know where you stand with them and make sure they know where they stand with you.

To all my fake friends I said goodbye. I have

always been the type of friend that would give my last. I love hard because it's the only way I know how. If I can keep you out of harm's way, I will. But what I have learned is that you cannot expect that everyone else's idea of a friend is the same as yours. Sometimes, being a friend means accepting the flaws you see and loving them anyway, but from a safe, respectful distance Love endures.

Of course, I have friends that truly care about me and have my best interest at heart. I can always tell by the way they sympathize with me, embrace me and encourage me through every moment, even if it's telling me I was not right about something. No matter the situation, my closest friends have been with me through thick and thin. I love them dearly and I consider them my family now. Some friendships do come to an end, but the family we've built will last forever.

Strategies for pulling back the layers of unhealthy friendships start with identifying who is for you and who is not. Proximity or length of time are not determining factors for the quality of a friendship. Really look at it from the perspective of do they listen to you, give you wise counsel, do they push you to better, etc. Determine what type of friendships you'd like to have. Past situations may have you desiring trustworthiness, support, and availability. And by availability, I mean, they are intentional about making time for you. Once you're able to assess the type of friendships you'd like to establish, you must also identify the types of friendships you currently have. Using the criteria, you'd like in a friend, make sure the people around you support your dreams and goals and do not negatively impact or hinder your growth.

Be careful of the bad habits your friends keep. Submitting to the influences of others bad habits can also lead you to a road of bad habits that can be very hard to shake, such as drugs or extreme alcohol consumption. You may have even been told that these habits will ease your pain and make you feel better. We need to look at the friendships that promote false realities, cover-ups, an in-the-moment fixes. Our friendships should push us to be better or at minimum not demean or diminish our worth and integrity. What we cannot afford is to allow are ourselves to be privy to environments, relationships or situations that create an unstable state of mind, depression or worse. We are called to be a light and an influence in the kingdom of God. Our friends should reflect and illuminate our light to be brighter. Shine on!

Sometimes conflicts will rear its ugly head. Falling out with your friends may be inevitable, but you have to be willing to forgive yourself and others. Often times we are our biggest critic. You may or may not be to blame for the disagreement. If you are, admit it. Apologize, because your friendship is worth more than your pride. Even if you are not to blame, try to communicate effectively and resolve the issue. The same requirements you have of your friends, you must be as well. Don't let a disagreement or petty words come between you. As mentioned about the relationship with your spouse, your mouth speaks what's in your heart.

If you're a true, sincere friend, you would never want them to be scarred by you as you have from others. It is not okay, to let your friend leave your life, without them knowing that you are sorry, you miss them and that you cherish your friendship. An apology will go a long way to fostering conversation, forgiveness and reconciliation. When we don't do these things, we start hating ourselves. We reflect on things others have done to us or things we have done to ourselves and regret what has taken place. You feed what you focus on. Hate and regret will not change things. They are already done. But, if left un-atoned for, they can fester and grow. Eventually, you will turn on yourself.

When we cannot or will not forgive ourselves, we begin to feel upset. We'll continually recap the argument or words we said to each other and beat ourselves up. We become our own worst enemy by holding on and not forgiving ourselves or others. You have to make peace with the situation. If you hold on to these things forever the healing process is not possible. Most mistakes can be healed with forgiveness whether it is for self, others or a situation. By doing this you also unleash the layer of unforgiveness and free yourself to be that much closer to healing.

Spending personal time with those you love also aids you in peeling back the layers of unhealthy friendships as well. How? Because it promotes better relationships and bonds which are priceless. There are so many activities that you and your friends can do to bond. Some examples are having a pot luck with your friends instead of spending money at restaurants, movie or game nights. Invite friends over for a better connection. Have an intimate gathering instead of going to a happy hour.

Another way to be a better friend, you need to be your own best friend. By spending time with yourself it helps you identify the areas in your life that need healing. When you consider that hurt people hurt people, you have to realize that you are the first person that you hurt. Consider this:

- Do you neglect yourself?
- Do you ignore your inner thoughts or red flags?
- Do you demean yourself?
- Do you acknowledge your wants or needs?

Chances are if you are willing to do this to yourself, then you may either project or siphon your closest relationships of love and positivity for want of fulfilling these deficits. Once you truly have a quality relationship with yourself, you'll be better equipped to determine what type of friend you'd like coming from the perspective of being your own best friend, aligns you to take better care of yourself. It protects you from attracting and developing the wrong types of relationships with people who are not interested or invested in seeing you live your best life.

In this section, I challenge you to look closely at the friendships you have. There are so many levels to relationships. Are any of them one-sided? Are there people you call friends who should really be acquaintances or associates? Setting boundaries and knowing where you stand with others are important. Do a thorough self-examination to find out if you are truly being a friend to someone. Equally, you should identify if the parameters of your individual friendships need to be redefined. Be honest in your assessment, because the result will be friendships that will pass the test of time.

Here are some helpful things to consider when developing and maintaining healthy friendships:

Love Yourself

When you take the time out to be your own best friend, you can learn to forgive yourself and accept yourself for any imperfections. You also have an opportunity to look within yourself and to find out who you really are. When becoming your own best friend and loving yourself ensure that the relationship you have with yourself is a positive one. As time goes on the love you give to yourself will pour out on those around you. Allowing you to treat people the same way you would desire to be treated.

Beware Social Media Traps

In today's day and age people tend to spend more time looking down at their phones instead of paying attention to the person that's right in front of their face. Don't get so caught up in posting on social media that you forget how to hold a basic conversation or begin to ignore your friends in real life.

Listen Effectively

Listening is a crucial skill in boosting another person's self-esteem, the silent form of flattery that makes people feel supported and valued. Listening and understanding what others communicate to us is the most important part of successful interaction and vice versa.

Be an Active Listener

Active or reflective listening is the single most useful and important listening skill. In active listening, we also are genuinely interested in understanding what the other person is thinking, feeling, wanting, or what the message means, and we are active in checking out our understanding before we respond with our own new message.

Give Your Time

Giving time to people is also a huge gift. In a world where time is of the essence and we are trying to fit in more than one lifetime, we don't always have the time to give to our loved ones, friends, and work colleagues. Being present in the time you give to people is also important, so that, when you are with someone, you are truly with someone and not dwelling in the past or worrying about the future.

Develop Your Communication Skills

Develop and work on your communication skills. One of the biggest dangers with communication is that we can work on the assumption that the other person has understood the message we are trying to get across.

Learn To Give and Take Feedback

From your own personal perspective, any feedback you receive is free information and you can choose whether you want to take it on board or not. It can help you to tap into your blind spot and get a different perspective.

Questions to assist you with unleashing your layers:

Who is someone you trust, who could provide valuable insight into your situations as they arise?

_____

_____

_____

_____

_____

_____

_____

_____

Do you invest as much quality time with yourself as you do with others?

_____

_____

_____

_____

_____

_____

What characteristics do you look for in a person you are considering becoming friends with?

_____

_____

_____

_____

_____

_____

Have you evaluated the people around you, you consider friends? If so, do they add value to your life? In what ways do they add value?

_____

_____

_____

_____

_____

_____

_____

Do you feel as though you receive as much as you give in your friendships?

_____

_____

_____

_____

_____

_____

How do overcome conflicts in friendships?

_____

_____

_____

_____

_____

_____

_____

What boundaries have you set with your friends to ensure you have a healthy relationship?

_____

_____

_____

_____

_____

_____

How much time have you spent developing a relationship with you?

_____

_____

_____

_____

_____

_____

_____

_____

I continue to believe that if children are given the necessary tools to succeed, they will succeed beyond their wildest dreams!

- David Vitter

Unleashing The Layers of Children

When we create a new life, we produce a being that contains parts of each of us. Not only do our children receive our physical features and good character, but they also inherit some of our dysfunctions and bad habits. As they grow into their personalities you will begin to identify these things as a parent. As you realize the dysfunction and bad habits, the first thing you have to do is face these things within yourself. You cannot expect your children to do things that you are unwilling to do. You cannot ask your children to search their souls if you will not do the same.

Once you're able to correct these things within you, it enables you to do the same with your children. We have to be the change we want to see. Our children will follow our example and will be able to break a generational cycle. This is what truly allows us to set our children up for success that far exceeds finances. Often, we only see what we do to provide for our children as a means of success. However, when we peel back our layers of dysfunction and become better people, we have to ask ourselves a question: Are we truly making an impact on our children and the future generations that follow?

What are we teaching them and what are they simply learning by our example? We must be willing to do the research if we don't know instead of expecting our children to find out on their own. When we know better, we should do better. The legacy we pass down to our children should be a richer, more fulfilling life than what we had.

Once I entered motherhood myself, I better understood all that was required to be not only a woman but a mother. I'm so thankful for being blessed to give birth to a beautiful daughter and a wonderful son. Motherhood is one of the most important roles I have had to play, but it definitely has had its challenges.

As a baby develops within you, a special bond is formed. It forced me to look at relationships and life completely different. I never knew that I could feel love like this before. It may have been because I often wondered if my mother loved me. But my experience was special. Every month that went by allowed my affection to grow deeper for my children. It caused me to stretch in ways I didn't know were possible, but it required that I peel back the layers that I didn't know existed.

My kids are the greatest version of myself. My kids and I are unbreakable. My son has been around the longest and has been there with me through my highs and lows. I love the bond that we share. My daughter is my twin, just a smaller version of me. I found that the connection I wanted with my sisters, God gave to me with my daughter. The love and protection of my son reminds me of my father and how much of a protector he was. I think I share a bit of that as a parent also. I'm thankful that as I improve, my children's future does too. I had to grow up and learn how to be responsible. I also learned how to be a role model for someone else. That taught me how to care for another person more than myself. I'm grateful for them pushing me to become the woman that I am today.

When you give birth to children, they push you to be a better person as a whole. You are driven to provide for them everything you may not have had. You want to protect them from the hurt and disappointment you've faced and put them in position to succeed in life. It requires putting aside your own selfish desires to care for the life of another. In order to do so I had to push past what I didn't know and experience and learn how to love all over again.

I'm really not sure that I even learned how to love growing up. I desired love and affection from my parents. I wished that I had a close bond with my siblings but neither seemed to be the case. The affection I longed for as I child really took a toll on me and impacted my attitude towards people and relationships. Though I desired affection it was something foreign to me.

I committed to ensuring that my kids wouldn't

have to go through wondering if I loved them or desiring to have affection from me. However, you learn that your love may not be enough to fulfill a child's heart, especially when one parent is absent. I became aware that no matter how much I gave of me, great things and awesome experiences; it would never be enough to fill the void of what a child really desires or wants. This has and is still the hardest part of parenthood for me. As a child of mine, if their heart hurts so does mine. I wanted them to have all the memories that I never got to cherish. Now, being on the other end of the spectrum – from child to parent – I now identify with how my mother must have felt. It is difficult sometimes to reconcile in my mind, now that the shoe is on the other foot; that my child may now feel about me how I felt about my mother.

It made me strive to go above and beyond, but the hardest part of it all was having to dig into all the feelings. There were broken pieces that I still had left unresolved from childhood. Even with my issues I knew I didn't want to pass them down to my children. I had to be real with myself which was painful. However, it wasn't as painful as the thought of having my children grow up wondering whether or not I loved them. So, I had a choice to make. Either I could do what my family did and make everything look good from the outside. Or, I could do the work to make sure my children's lives looked good inside and out.

As you look at the reflections of yourself, you have to take the highs and the lows with it all. I had to understand that my children were here with purpose and had to grow in their own ways. Not always has this been easy, but I realize it's my job to see it through. As hard as you might work to give your children the lives you think they ought to have, it's ultimately up to them to decide how they are going to live. Parenting is hard work and it's not for everyone. But, if you chose to give birth then you chose to be a parent. You now owe it to your children to be the best one you can be.

In this section, take a deep look at yourself and decide what kind of parent you have been and what kind of parent you want to be. If you're on track, then keep going. If you need to make some changes then now's the time!

Here are some helpful things to consider as you unleash the layers of parenting children:

Know Your Strengths

Face it you are an imperfect parent. You have strengths and weaknesses as a family leader. Try to have realistic expectations for yourself, your spouse, and your kids. You don't have to have all the answers — be forgiving of yourself. Focus on the areas that need the most attention rather than trying to address everything all at once. Admit it when you're burned out. Take time out from parenting to do things that will make you happy as a person or as a couple.

Lead By Example

Being a good role model for your children is extremely important because children emulate what they see. Lead by example and guide them towards a successful future.

Boosting Your Child's Self-Esteem

Boosting a child's self-esteem when they're young gives them the confidence they need to thrive in life and venture out to try new things. Establishing self-esteem early on also help children cope with mistakes and try to do their best in everything they do.

Reward Your Child/Children for Their Good Behavior

When you reward your child/children with good behavior you will repeat that same behavior they received positive feedback and avoid behaviors that don't generate any rewards. Rewards also build a child's confidence. Confident children are more likely to follow their parents' direction, take pride in their achievements and develop social skills that will benefit them throughout their lives.

Set Limits and Be Consistent With Your Discipline

Setting limits and being consistent with your discipline can help to reduce stress in family relationships and make parenting easier. Children need to know what you expect of them in order to behave appropriately. This helps them understand the value of having rules and motivates them to cooperate. For example, you might discuss as a family the sorts of rules that will help you all get on well together. These might include things like talking to each other rather than shouting, asking before borrowing things, putting away games and toys after playing with them, or taking a turn to wash up after dinner.

Make Communication a Priority

It's important as a parent to keep the communication channels open by being patient and understanding. If your child feels as if they aren't being heard they will shut down and shut you out of their lives.

There Is No Right or Wrong Way to Parenting

There are moments in parenting when you may question whether or not you're doing things the right way. However, there's no right no wrong way to parent a child. You have to do what's best for you and your family. Just be flexible and willing to adjust your parenting style as needed, so that it's beneficial to the development of your child. Show them that you love them unconditionally.

Questions to assist you with unleashing your layers:

What are some changes you experienced in becoming a parent?

_____

_____

_____

How has your upbringing impacted your parenting skills?

How has becoming a parent changed you?

_____

_____

_____

_____

_____

_____

_____

_____

What are some of the good qualities you see in your children?

_____

_____

_____

_____

_____

What layers are you unleashing to ensure your children have a better future?

Name 3 of your top parenting goals?

_____

_____

_____

_____

_____

_____

What are some characteristics you see in your child/children that are a reflection of you?

_____

_____

_____

_____

_____

_____

_____

_____

What you may not realize is that the words you say, and the words you hear from others have the power to change your entire life.

- Alex Uwajeh

Unleashing The Layers of the Tongue

We all have "problems" what differentiates the most successful people is how they approach them. You can't change the old news, but you can create good news. We have the power to manifest what we speak. Life and death lay in the tongue. Get in tune with yourself so that you can become aware of when you're speaking negatively and correct it.

Life consists of 10% what happens to you and 90% how you react to the situations that arise. When you change the way, you describe your "problems," it opens up whole new avenues for dealing with them. When we start to speak life into our situation, we encounter positive experiences. Choose to speak in ways that bring out your best and make you feel more positive about your ability to do what inspires you and to change what doesn't.

We have a tendency to continuously talk about the negative situations in our lives both mentally and verbally. However, instead of harping on a bad thought, replace it with a positive affirmation. Positive affirmations are positive statements aimed to affect the conscious and the subconscious mind which in turn, influences your behavior, habits, actions and reactions. By saying them, we are addressing something negative in our lives in a healthy way and putting a positive spin on it. You have to fully believe the words that are coming out of your mouth and use phrases that you know will steer you to a better outlook.

As you go about your day's activities be conscious of how you are talking to yourself in your mind. You have to believe that your attitude is everything. If your attitude is on the right temperature when issues arise, you have a better chance of addressing them better. It helps you conquer the most challenging issues with courage, grace and faith.

Learning to lean on your strength will take a lot of investing in your faith to believe better is coming. You can't face a challenge head on if you expect a negative outcome. You must choose to approach it knowing that this is only a phase to get you to the next point. Practice responding rather than reacting to a situation. You're probably asking what's the difference? Well, the difference is you're conditioning yourself to think before you speak instead of simply reacting to a situation and blurting stuff out. Take it from me, my filter unleashed many times, it was things others were thinking, but I had the courage to say. Sometimes it was in the right place and sometimes not.

As you grow in developing your attitude and mindset towards life's transitions, you'll be able to respond with more of a conscious thought instead of an immediate reaction. Believe it or not each time we respond to something we are making a conscious choice on how we are going to react to it. We think before we open our mouths. A solid support system is a good start with helping you move towards a better you for the present and future.

New positive experiences can bring you into a greater scenario to a point where you only focus your attention on things that bring you peace. If you can vow to think life and speak life, it will set you up and prepare you for any obstacle that you may face from here on out. You will have energy like no other! Your approach to a situation when you hear it and face it will allow the load to be less heavy.

We were born with strength that we must continue to let lead us through what can be an even greater life. As we all know, there will always be someone who will try to throw sticks and stones to tear us down. In these times let your courage, grace and faith supersede their tactics. You are now on a new level of success!

You have the power to speak your own healing into existence. Forming healthy relationships, strong family bonds and a successful future are possible. Your marriage and your children are strong, and you have obtained financial stability for yourself and the next generation. The bible says, *speak those things that be not as though they were.* Now is the time to **SPEAK LIFE!!!**

Here are some helpful tips to remember as you are transforming your words and thoughts to create a better life for yourself:

Adjust Your Attitude

Start your day with positive affirmations. Your attitude directly affects your mindset so begin by adjusting your attitude towards everything that has taken place. Some studies show that personality traits such as optimism and pessimism can affect many areas of your health and well-being. The positive thinking that usually comes with optimism is a key part of effective stress management. And effective stress management is associated with many health benefits.

Make Love Notes to Yourself

Dealing with our feelings about our lives, reflecting on how we truly feel about ourselves, and encouraging ourselves to be kinder and more compassionate can lead to healing, happiness and even better health. Make a list of positive power words or phrases. Write them out. Post them where you will see them then say them out loud each time you pass one.

Focus On the Positive

If you are a person who continuously speaks negativity every time a situation occurs practice turning negative self-talk into positive self-talk until it becomes second nature to you. Start by finding something positive to focus on in the midst of every bad situation you're faced with no matter how small it may seem. By doing this you will increase your lifespan, decrease your depressive episodes if you have any, develop a better psychological and physical well-being, as well as develop better coping skills during hardships and times of stress.

Take Your Day Back

Periodically during the day, stop and evaluate what you're thinking. No matter how difficult your day may be if you find that your thoughts are mainly negative, try to find a way to put a positive spin on them. Then find one positive point to focus on. Be sure to look for the lesson in everything you go through. This will help you get through the difficult moments.

Multiply Positivity

We all have our strategies for dealing with hard days and rough times so it's good to surround yourself with positive people to draw inspiration from during your rough moments. There's an old saying that we become like those we choose to hold closest. Therefore, it's worth the time it may take to consciously surround you with people who can create goodness for themselves, and those around them.

Questions to assist you with unleashing your layers:

When faced with difficulty, do you find yourself speaking positively or negatively about the situation?

Has your speech impacted your situation?

What methods or tools do you use to maintain a positive mindset?

List 5 affirmations you can speak daily?

Message From the Author

Listen, life occurs daily. It comes with uncontrollable and controllable moments. Identify what does and does not matter in life and make the best of them both. Overcome your trials with all the strength you possess. Even if you are not feeling confident, dig deep, it is inside of you. All you need is faith the size of a mustard seed and you can conquer anything. Take it from me, I came, saw, conquered and am still conquering some of the same obstacles as you. *"Whatever you do, work at it with all your heart as working for the Lord, not for human masters" Colossians 2:23.*

Remember, this is your life and you should live it according to God's plan. Others who feel they are in a better situation than you are, can make you feel less than or not qualified. But, you should always remain positive and do what works for you. We can't dwell on what others say, think or feel all the time. Enjoying simple things allows you to appreciate the bigger things when it's time. Remember, you must be your biggest cheerleader, motivator, innovator and much more. Your inner you, must be the best of you.

I challenge you to unleash the layers of your life that have been holding you in bondage and keeping you from embracing the light that shines within you.

Unleash the layer of bondage!
Unleash the pain!

Layers Unleashed

Unleash the guilt!
Unleash the layer of sisterhood!
Unleash the layer of betrayal!
Unleash the layer of intention!
Unleash the layer of resentment!
Unleash the layer of fake friends!
Unleash your layer of discomfort!
Unleash your layer of abuse!
Unleash your layers of friendships!
Unleash your layers of finance!
Unleash your layers of darkness!
Unleash your layers of grief!
Unleash your layers of the tongue!

Notes:

Layers Unleashed

Layers Unleashed

www.ingramcontent.com/pod-product-compliance
Lightning Source LLC
Chambersburg PA
CBHW050501240426
43673CB00023B/452/J